Scheduling: The Secret to Homeschool Sanity

Plan Your Way Back to Mental Health

Lee Binz,
The HomeScholar

First Printing, 2014

Printed in the United States of America

Cover Design by Robin Montoya
Edited by Kimberly Charron

ISBN: 1500412309
ISBN-13: 978-1500412302

Disclaimer: Parents assume full responsibility for the education of their children in accordance with state law. College requirements vary, so make sure to check with the colleges about specific requirements for homeschoolers. We offer no guarantees, written or implied, that the use of our products and services will result in college admissions or scholarship awards.

Scheduling - The Secret to Homeschool Sanity

Plan Your Way Back to Mental Health

If you want to incorporate more scheduling into your homeschool but don't feel capable of implementing it yourself, use a curriculum that comes with assignment sheets already created for you.

Put Weak Areas First

One of the best ways to save your sanity in the midst of homeschooling is to put your weak area first. Invest your resources wisely in two ways: money and time.

Putting your weak area first in terms of money means spending more money in that area. If math is your weak area, it's where you spend more money. Sometimes this means you will also need to re-spend money. If a curriculum isn't working, and it's your weak area, be willing to try again with a different curriculum.

You also want to invest your time first in your weak area. Your weak subject should be the first thing you work on in your homeschool, no matter what happens. It's what you commit to doing with your child before you have fun for the rest of your day.

Invest in Yourself

Homeschooling is your chosen profession and investing in yourself is important, much like professional teachers take continuing education classes. Take what you need to help you do your job seriously. Think of it as an investment. If you have a weak area, invest in yourself so you can do your best.

Hold a Morning Meeting

A morning meeting with your child is a daily investment in your personal mental health and sanity. Your ultimate goal as a homeschool parent is to become the project manager rather than the teacher, especially as your child gets into the high school years.

Hold a quick, daily check-in as the project manager. It doesn't have to be a long check-in, merely enough to make sure your kids know what they're going to do for the day, and whether they did their job the previous day. Using an assignment sheet can provide some structure for your morning meeting. You can use a checklist for subjects such as math and English.

A daily morning meeting can help your child grow in responsibility. As homeschoolers, our goal is for our children to become independent and responsible. Don't expect them to become 100% independent and responsible on the first day of high school. It takes all four years of high school to train teenagers to become as independent as adults, and that still may not happen even after they're seniors.

Having a morning meeting may not be universal, but even in the working world people don't function 100%

independently. Most people have regular check-ins with their employers and staff. Even people who work from home have regular check-in meetings with others. Use this opportunity to help your teen along the path to independence.

Chapter 2

Sharing Responsibilities

There are two different kinds of responsibilities within a homeschool: the sharing of household tasks and the sharing of homeschool tasks. Both are important. Anything other family members can do for you or in your place can remove responsibilities from you as the primary teacher and make your job easier.

The more help you get around the home, the more likely you are to be successful. Every time somebody else unloads the dishwasher, it's ten minutes of your day back! It's important to share these responsibilities, even with young children. When they pick up the table or sweep the floor, it's one more thing you don't have to do, giving you more hours in your day.

Older Children

Whether you have a large or small family, it's important to remember that older children can help younger children. It's well documented that this enhances learning, and can help everyone. If an older child helps a younger one with history or math, it will firm up the older child's skills as well.

Teaching others also develops responsibility. Older children can take responsibility for the younger child, babysitting for an hour while you do household or homeschool tasks (or go out to dinner with your spouse)!

Younger Children

It can be hard to keep the youngest entertained while doing homeschool work with older children. Try using activity boxes to keep the little ones occupied. Fill them with fun and educational activities your child can happily and quietly play with on their own. Spend some of your summer time or free time preparing these activity boxes, and rotate them each day or week. This makes them much more appealing to your child, who will be eager to see the new box each time, and frees your time up to focus your attention elsewhere.

You can also rotate assigned playtime. Assign a younger child to an older sibling for a morning hour and perhaps another older sibling for an afternoon hour. By rotating playtime, they won't get tired of each other, but it will still increase your amount of free time to complete your work.

Young kids do need some time alone for unstructured play. Keep your young child's activities varied, and don't expect them to sit quietly and color the whole day long while you teach older siblings.

As you consider how to include your young children in your daily routine, I encourage you to think about your goal, which is to increase their love of learning and love of homeschooling. Although it's nice for them to have a coloring sheet to work on while they're listening to read-alouds, you don't want the younger ones to sit in chairs and do school for many hours a day and get burned out. You want them to develop a love of learning that will last for years.

Create Margin

Margin is an important concept for sanity in your homeschool. It means there's enough room in your schedule to allow for some down time or free time. Allow enough margin for unplanned interruptions, so your day won't be ruined. If your mother knocks on your door for a cup of tea, margin will allow you to accommodate that interruption. If you can give yourself even fifteen minutes of flextime each hour, your day will go more smoothly.

Margin means putting the big rocks into your "jar" first. Make sure the most important things go on your schedule first and the less important things are scheduled later. This way, you'll usually get the important things done.

The problem is that urgent things will sometimes seem important when they're not. If you keep doing the urgent thing time after time, you will only be putting out fires and making no progress. Instead, schedule the important things first, such as weak subject areas and core courses, and you'll make some real progress.

Meals can also benefit from rotation. If you rotate meals each day of the week for dinner, it's not as much work, especially if you have the same meal every Monday, Tuesday, etc.

For dinners, some families rotate the same meal each day of the month. For instance, on the first day of the month they might have tacos, and on the second day they might have roast chicken. Other families rotate a menu theme, each Tuesday having Italian food on the menu, and each Friday, fish, for example.

Rotate chores as well. Some need to be done every hour and others need to be done daily, weekly, or monthly. You can also rotate chores by who's responsible for each one.

For homeschool work with Mom, it can be useful to rotate through so each child gets your individual attention.

Cover Core Curriculum

Make sure you cover the core classes: reading, writing, math, and science. Sometimes core classes are hard to include in your day, especially if they're not your child's favorite subjects. Delight directed subjects (what your child does because they like the activity), are easier to get done. It's easy to miss a core subject here or there if you're not paying attention.

One way to stay on top of core subjects is to make sure you don't leave home for the day until they are finished. I have talked to many homeschoolers who used this strategy with their children; when a child wanted to go out and play, they could play as soon as the core curriculum was done. I know one homeschooler who got up at 5 in the morning each day to get his core curriculum done, so he would be finished everything by 11 AM and have the rest of the day to study his passion—

chess.

Quiet Time

Set aside some quiet time for yourself. It is an important part of keeping a sane schedule. Schedule time for projects and fun—maybe that's when you do your sewing, quilting, scrapbooking, or reading for pleasure. Even 30 minutes of relaxation working on something you enjoy can improve your outlook. For Christian homeschoolers, it's also important to have a quiet time with God to prioritize and get yourself centered.

Kids also need quiet time. They need down time alone in their room (and not plugged in to any digital media). Alone time allows for creative thinking.

Margin and quiet time is critical to everyone's sanity. Most homeschoolers are so busy with everything we do in our lives that there seems to be no time for us to sit down, catch our breath, and have a quiet moment.

Bite-sized Bits

The big pieces of life overwhelm homeschool parents sometimes. If that happens to you, try to organize your activities in bite-sized bits. Think about it this way: you can spend 10 minutes on laundry each hour—that would be all you need to rotate the laundry, put in the next load, and take out the dry load. When school is over, you can get the folding done. Ten minutes is all you need to put dinner in a crock-pot so you have a hot meal at the end of the day. Ten minutes might be all you need for a quick pick-up before Dad comes home, to make sure the house isn't a complete disaster.

Making goals is a great idea, but it's important not to get overwhelmed by those goals. Some people set aside one day for doing laundry, and end up not being able to cope with the huge laundry load. Spend ten minutes every hour instead and you'll get it done.

.

Chapter 4

Benefits of Scheduling

There are many benefits to scheduling. Even if you don't see yourself as a scheduler, you can still provide a framework for your day and keep your unique routines.

Think about your schedule as a recipe for gingerbread cookies. A gingerbread cookie recipe doesn't have to result in all the cookies looking like gingerbread men. Some cookies could be gingerbread birds, some could have frosting all over them, and some could have less frosting.

Schedules are like recipes. A schedule gives you a backbone to work with, but it doesn't have to be rigorous or restrictive. It can increase your flexibility and productivity, which will help you feel happier in your job and reduce your stress, because you will feel like you're getting something done.

A schedule can smooth out the bumps in your day, because you can allot 15 minutes every hour for any crisis which may happen. When the grape juice spills on the floor, you already have 15 minutes of flextime planned so you can clean up. Scheduling has more benefits than a smoothly running day. It can also help develop good work habits in your child, so they understand how to plan their lives when they're an adult.

Remember that a schedule is only a framework to get things done and not a taskmaster. If you have a meal scheduled for dinner, even if it's frozen pizza, and someone suggests going out for dinner, you can drop the pizza and go. Because it's scheduled doesn't mean you must have it for dinner, or that you have to clean something thoroughly every week. It's a "serving suggestion" like those found in a recipe book or grocery store flyers.

Daily Schedule

The specifics of creating a daily schedule involve putting your priorities first. Keep the daily schedule as similar as possible on a day-to-day basis. If you go to your co-op every Tuesday morning, all your afternoons will look the same but your mornings may include either co-op, or art and science (because they're project-based).

If your child has piano lessons on Friday afternoons, you might decide to schedule reading every afternoon. Alternatively, every afternoon during the week could be when your child does independent work.

You can create different kinds of schedules. One could be for activity days when you're out and about. Use it for co-op days, and days you do grocery shopping or your child has piano lessons.

A second schedule could be for when you're at home all day, working on home activities and core subjects. Use whatever schedules work best for your family's unique situation.

How to Create a Schedule

Before you create a schedule, create a list first. What does the parent need to do? What does the student need to do? Remember that not all tasks are sequential; the student can perform a task at the same time as the parent is accomplishing something.

Ask yourself when you need to work together. Be careful with the word *need*, because sometimes you don't need to teach or even help your child. Think about what your child can do independently and make it a goal to get your child working more independently by the end of the year.

As you begin to implement your schedule, work out what time family members will do each task. Use 30-minute intervals, because some subjects don't take a whole hour. Math might take two 30-minute periods, but independent reading time only one.

Use different color sticky notes for each family member's jobs or responsibilities, sticking them on a paper time chart to figure out how everything will fit together. It's possible to do this on a computer, but with all the cutting and pasting of information, it's easy to lose something. You might forget to paste after cutting, and all of a sudden it's gone and you've forgotten to put an important task on the schedule.

I prefer making the schedule on paper, then transferring it to a computer, printing it out, and discussing it as a family. One of the problems I had with scheduling was getting excited by all the pretty colors and forgetting to share the schedule with my family! That doesn't work, because your family won't stick to the schedule, and do it independently unless you tell them ahead of time!

Scheduling Resource

The book, *Managers of Their Homes*, covers scheduling and assignments for homeschool families and is written from a Christian perspective. I found it extremely helpful, even though I had two compliant children. The author of the book had eight children when she wrote it, so it is particularly helpful for large families and those with wide age ranges.

In the book, Teri Maxwell talks about raising teenagers and babies at the same time—two in diapers, a fifteen-year-old, a thirteen-year-old, and everything in between. Even though I only had two children, and neither child was far outside the box, I got so much out of this book.

When my niece started homeschooling, I loaned her the book, and she was not willing to give it back for about a year! Even though I haven't homeschooled for many years, I still love *Managers of Their Homes*. It gives me comfort simply to look at the cover of the book.

When my children were freshmen, my daily schedule included one column for Mom, one column for Alex, and one column for Kevin. It included a different time for each of us to wake up and have our quiet time. It certainly took me longer to dress and shower than it did my young boys.

We all came together for activities we needed to do as a group: foreign language and read aloud time. Then I tutored one child while the other worked on the Latin textbook, and then we switched. Later, they worked independently, and we came together again to have lunch. In the afternoon, they worked independently on piano practice or biology. I also made sure to schedule some free time for both my children and me. If they finished the chores, they could enjoy some free time.

That's what my homeschool day looked like. You will come up with the right schedule for your own homeschool, because every family is different.

Scheduling Tips

If you're overwhelmed by scheduling, start with school hours. These hours are more routine than after school hours, when you're off to soccer practice or church.

Start scheduling with only the core subjects, such as math, science, and foreign language, in order to finish by lunchtime. If you can schedule chores along with schoolwork, then your child will understand that learning and chores are part of life—both go hand in hand, and will always be important to them. It can also help your home run more smoothly.

Give your children a chance to give input on their schedules—especially older kids. One year, I created a schedule but my son Kevin wanted it a different way. I gave him the Word document and he created his own schedule.

Things will change over time—maybe you'll finish a class, stop co-op classes, or can't avoid piano anymore. It's important to update your schedule regularly, especially if you have a baby. Babies grow and change, and suddenly you will find they don't take their morning nap anymore, which can make things difficult! Try to remain flexible.

Chapter 5

How to Avoid a Crazy Busy Life in Seven Easy Steps

You may think the toddler age is the busiest stage of life you'll ever experience, but it's not true. The busy season builds again during high school, culminating in the maniacal rush through college admission. The maximum busy season is senior year of high school, when the consequences are financial and huge.

The crazy busy life can be avoided. And you can begin immediately by instituting calming policies right away. You simply need to know how to avoid the crazy

peace filled life. Teach them not to lose track of the important things. This is a life skill, like learning to drive or doing laundry.

3. Meditate on Scripture

People think parenting babies and toddlers is the hardest time of life. I know I did—I had one *difficult* baby in Alex! But now I see that homeschooling high school is even busier. Crazy busy parents have a hard time being self-controlled, pure, or kind, and it's hard to be obedient to the Word of God in the midst of chaos.

Christian women are usually of two camps. Either they are a balanced "Mary" or a completely overwhelmed "Martha," complaining about their busy life. Jesus points out that Mary chose the better way.

> Mary, who sat at the Lord's feet listening to what he said. But Martha was distracted by all the

preparations that had to be made . . . "Martha, Martha," the Lord answered, "you are worried and upset about many things, but few things are needed—or indeed only one. Mary has chosen what is better, and it will not be taken away from her." Luke 10:38-42.

Christian women look to the example of the Proverbs 31 woman, forgetting it is the culmination of a lifetime of accomplishment, rather than a week in the life of a human being. Spend some time meditating on scriptures about rest and spend time with God. "Come to me, all you who are weary and burdened, and I will give you rest." Matthew 11:28

Recognize how the Scriptures emphasize rest.

There are six days when you may work, but the seventh day is a day of Sabbath rest, a day of sacred assembly. You are not to do any work. Leviticus 23

There are consequences if we don't rest, and He will make us lie down.

The Lord is my shepherd, I lack nothing. He makes me lie down in green pastures, he leads me beside quiet waters, he refreshes my soul. Psalm 23:1-3

When I was working as a nurse, I often saw the result of over-scheduling. It's true we should work. It says so in the Old Testament, "The Lord God took the man and put him in the Garden of Eden to work it and take care of it." Genesis 2:15. And it says so in the New Testament, "Jesus said to them, 'My Father is always at his work to this very day, and I too am working.'" John 5:17

And we often work so hard for a good reason—it's fulfilling! It says so in the Old Testament, "A sluggard's appetite is never filled, but the desires of the diligent are fully satisfied." Proverbs 13:4. And it's explained again in the New Testament, "Whatever you do, work at it with all your heart, as working for the Lord, not for human masters." Colossians 3:23.

But we are called to alternate rest and work. Even farmland is to alternate rest and work, as the Bible talks about the "Sabbath Year" in Leviticus 25:4-7. We are called to rest. The Lord instructs us to plan ahead to rest. It's not optional.

We are called to be busy *at home*, not busy for the sake of being crazy-busy.

> Urge the younger women to love their husbands and children, to be self-controlled and pure, to be busy at home, to be kind, and to be subject to their husbands, so that no one will malign the word of God. Titus 2: 4-5.

eventually participate independently in activities. Simply remember that independence doesn't happen overnight. It's a process that takes years, with lots of training, modeling, and encouragement. And along with independence, you are working to form family closeness to last a lifetime.

Are you expecting too much?

Some parents expect their children to do school for more hours than the average adult's work day. When you add after school activities, it leaves no time for relaxation or even catching your breath. It's too much! Scale back and limit homeschool work to a reasonable amount for each subject, with core classes first. Add a reasonable amount of activities that still allow for free time as well.

Did you overestimate mornings?

While we would all like to say we get up at 6:00 AM to start our day, people rarely bound out of bed and work non-stop until midnight. If your homeschool plans are dependent on making a night owl into a morning person, it won't work. Don't overestimate what time you and your children become functional each morning, or how late you can stay coherent in the evening.

Can they concentrate that long?

Schools have 50-minute classes because studies show this is how long a teenager can concentrate. Studies also show that mixing physical activity breaks with seatwork increases productivity. Allow a balance between subjects and activities, so your child isn't asked to do seatwork for more than an hour at a time.

Could you do it as an adult?

This is a great way to assess your child's workload. If I told you to sit still, without moving, and pay attention to a computer screen or textbook for eight hours straight, and then run to soccer for three hours, could you do it? I don't think so! If you couldn't or shouldn't complete your plan as an adult, don't ask your child to do so, either.

5. Plan for Margin

Margin is the empty white space in a book that makes it more readable. Margin is also unplanned white space in life that makes life more livable. Instead of being completely overwhelmed by everything going on in your life right now, plan margin into your day. Set up unplanned free time and you are planning margin into your life.

Sleep is required to help your brain recover after a day of work. In a similar way, unplanned time allows the soul to recover. Children need free time to play and teens need free time to develop their individual interests. Parents need free time for sanity. But to achieve margin, you have to say "no" to many good things in life. Focus on leading a sane life. Sanity comes from margin.

6. Learn to Say "No"

Homeschoolers are caregivers, trying to teach kindness to their children. It can be difficult to say "no" when caregiving is in your DNA. Put your priorities first: children and family. Teach your children how to say no politely, so people listen. This assertiveness is valued in college, careers, and interpersonal relationships.

Not everyone has the "assertiveness gene" but saying "no" can be taught. There are three easy steps to saying no. The key is to express it as a "No Sandwich." Start with the word *no*, add an explanation or humor, and then end with the word *no* again. The other person will hear you this way, but without taking offense. Here is the formula for saying no.

Step 1: Say it. Start with a clear, simple, unambiguous declarative statement that nobody could possibly misunderstand. Choose one of these statements: "No. Nope. Absolutely not. I can't."

Step 2: Explain it. Add a short explanation. While certainly not required, it can make your "no" more polite or easy to swallow. Choose one of these statements: "I'm honored, but I can't. I have other priorities right now. Sorry, my schedule is full."

Step 3: End the conversation and walk away. Sometimes your "no" statement is not clearly heard, so if a polite explanation doesn't end the conversation, try replying with humor. Choose one of these statements: "Are you serious? My life is crazy enough as it is! My brain is full, and I can't fit in one more thing."

Be firm if you aren't heard. You may need to sound firmer, or even harsh, to protect your precious family time. If there are any lingering doubts or you still feel pressured, give your answer one last time with this statement: "Listen to what I'm saying. The answer is no." Then quickly turn to leave, or send the email without any further comment.

7. Institute Calming Policies

A healthy family shares a commitment to each family member. They spend time together and communicate to resolve conflict. Family members express appreciation. They share a common faith. Healthy families teach coping skills to younger members.

The key to a healthy family does is not a huge activity list. It requires balance and communication. As you think through the coming year, try to institute calming policies so your time spent together creates happy memories, not screaming matches.

Have a regular family meeting to prioritize a limited number of activities. Choose activities that are meaningful to the participant. Avoid saying "you should" or "we should" outside these meaningful activities. Share regular meals together as a whole family whenever possible. Plan unscheduled hours with free and quiet time.

The Most Balanced Life Wins

Have you heard "The one with the most toys wins"? It's not true. And the family with the most activities doesn't win, either. True success is not keeping the craziest schedule. Success is a healthy, happy extended family in the future. Focus on a sane life, not a busy life.

A balanced life for an adult includes work, rest, leisure, and family. Teach each portion of a balanced life to your teen. You don't want them to grow up to become a workaholic, any more than you want them to become a couch potato. You want your young men and women to recognize the value of a balanced life.

Demonstrate balance. Teach them what a quality home life looks like. This means spending enough time at home to show the value of your life at home.

Chapter 6

Assignment Sheets

Assignment sheets are merely simple checklists for activities: whose responsibility it is, on which day, for which subject, and for which assignment. Unlike a schedule, an assignment sheet does not specify when the work should be done during the day. The child can check off each item when it's complete. I love assignment sheets because they helped me delegate some of my homeschool tasks to my husband.

I worked hard to create assignment sheets. During our morning meeting each morning, I told my children what was expected. At that point, it was up to them to check off each item as they went through the day.

When my husband came home from work, he helped the children look over the assignment sheets to see whether they'd completed what they were supposed to that day. We joked that he was the principal, but it was extremely helpful. This took the weight off me when I had to make dinner and set the table. If you have a larger family, an older child could go over checklists with younger students to make sure they checked everything off at the end of the day.

Creating an Assignment Sheet

Here are some helpful steps for creating an assignment sheet. First, make a list of classes and what each child needs to do. Then, decide how to divide up the work.

Textbooks are usually divided into 32 to 36 even sections, often because public schools are open 32 to 36 weeks over the school year. If your textbook is already divided this way, you know your child needs to complete one chapter per week. If there are 18 chapters, then they have two weeks to get each chapter done.

If it's not divided this way, or you're not using a textbook, then think about scheduling in terms of hours. For example, you could set aside half an hour to do vocabulary and spelling and another half an hour for writing. This will be one credit because it adds up to one hour each day.

Arrange the subjects on a page, one week to a page, so you can list each subject each day for the whole week. Some parents go a step further and list the times on each page so their child knows when to do each task. Alternatively, list things in the order to be done, with the weakest areas first. Then transfer this information to a computer document.

Assess your expectations. How long will each subject take? Add it all up to be sure you aren't planning too many hours of work each day. Discuss the assignment sheets with each student, so they know exactly what to do, and make sure they check the list every day.

For English, your assignment sheet might include which books and chapters your child should read. Include writing assignments and any other skills to practice, such as vocabulary worksheets or spelling lessons each day. For math, list the assigned lesson or textbook. List social studies, science, foreign language, and any electives in the same way.

Remember that your schedule will be unique, because different families us different curriculum. Do whatever works for your family. One year, I made assignment sheets for one month at a time, and I also tried one year at time. It was bulky—hard to check things off, hard for me to see, and frankly, it was hard for my children to read my mind about exactly what they needed to do each day. I think one week at a time is the right amount of information for an assignment sheet, but you can try other lengths of time and see what works best in your homeschool.

High School Assignment Tips

As I've mentioned earlier, plan your core classes first. Otherwise, three-quarters of the way through the school year you may realize that your child has only completed ten out of thirty-six math lessons (and you would not be the first homeschooler to realize this).

If your child wants to play the guitar all day long, it's not a waste of time. Try to keep them focused on core classes first, though. Delight directed learning counts as elective credit, so scoop up delight directed learning and put it on your child's transcript.

Delight directed learning also takes time, so make sure you plug it into your high school assignment sheet, so your child has time for enjoyable electives and not only difficult subjects.

Summer Assignment Tips

During summer, we did some schoolwork and used assignment sheets, but usually for no more than an hour and a half or two hours per day. We included short, bite-sized lessons. My children had to do these subjects completely independently because I found that, although they needed to keep some of their skills fresh, at the same time, I needed a break.

One of the reasons I made assignment sheets was so they knew exactly what they had to do each day of summer. We scheduled a bit of math review, which can keep those skills fresh and make a huge difference in the end. They also studied foreign language, and I would include some other short, independent classes, such as keyboarding or health.

Don't forget to work on your

homeschool records during the summer and spend some time planning for the coming year!

Chapter 7

Chores and Record Keeping

Scheduling chores is important. You don't have to do all the household chores alone; you can teach your child to help. It's important to train your child to help because it teaches them responsibility and it's training for adulthood. When you delegate chores, you are also showing your child how to delegate responsibilities, which is an adult skill. Make sure you have realistic expectations, though.

When scheduling chores, first list what to do, then when to do it, how often, and who can do it. You'll be amazed how much children can do! Create a master list to help you figure out who can do each task. Then you need to implement your list! You have to discuss it as a family with your child, train and demonstrate the chore techniques involved, and delegate responsibilities among family members as well.

Our family used the Sidetracked Home Executives system (the one FlyLady based her system on), which incorporates chore cards instead of a list. A woman once told me it was terrible that I was telling my men what chores to do, but my husband and two younger boys liked it. They each had a stack of five cards, and knew they needed to do those five chores—they appreciated the clarity. Make sure that whatever you do, it fits your family.

Keeping Homeschool Records

Scheduling and assignments are closely tied to homeschool records. Regularly updating homeschool records all through high school will keep you sane during college admission. These records are hard to complete in a last-minute panic, but relatively simple if you work on them regularly.

Remember to keep what is required by state law, along with what you need to create a transcript, course descriptions, and a reading list. Develop a strategy that will be useful to you.

Some people use planners, while others use a notebook. How do you know the correct record keeping method for you? The answer is, the method you will use. It's not important whether you purchase a planner or use notebook paper.

People ask me all the time if a certain planner is a good planner, what planner they should buy, whether it's okay to use a free planner or an independent planner, and what kind of planner they should use. It doesn't matter which one you own. What matters is that you use it.

There were many typos all over my

records! All that I wrote down were courses with tests or quizzes, and I included a percentage grade—that was it. I did not have a planner; I only used notebook paper and whatever pen was next to me. I used up old paper and kept it all in a notebook. It is not important to use a planner; it's important that you keep records!

If you need more help with record keeping, check out Appendix 1: "Cubbies, Tubbies, and Binder Queens."

Chapter 8

Meals

The key to a successful menu plan is repetition, so begin by listing your family's favorite meals. Sometimes people plan for two weeks at a time, while others plan four weeks at a time. Whatever you do, make sure you list favorite meals and rotate them as often as possible.

You may choose a theme for each day, such as: Mexican, Italian, or Asian. Alternatively, you may wish to list what kind of meal you'll have each day: beef, chicken, meatless, or fish. Whatever you choose, a simple rotation is often easiest.

If you choose eight of your favorite

meals for breakfast, and rotate them seven days a week, they would never land on the same day. Some people want to keep the same meal for each day of the week, but you can avoid this if you prefer. Remember that your meal plan is only a suggestion to make life easier for you. If you have a sudden desire to cook a gourmet meal, you have that freedom!

Freezer Cooking

Another strategy to help with homemaking tasks is freezer cooking. Freezer cooking doesn't necessarily mean having a gigantic cooking party once a month. You can do freezer cooking on a weekly, monthly, or occasional basis.

Store freezer meals in large gallon Ziploc bags laid flat, so you can fit 30 days of dinners into a regular stand up refrigerator freezer compartment! Even if you don't have a freezer in your garage, you can still do freezer cooking.

I used *The Freezer Cooking Manual* from 30 Day Gourmet. They have a holiday version with some great recipes that I use every single year.

Slow Cookers

A slow cooker is a great tool because you can prepare dinner in the morning. When you have 15 minutes of flex time, you can throw something in your crock-pot and have something to eat that night. It's a good idea to get a second crock-pot, so you can cook a meal for dinner and still have another crock-pot to do freezer cooking and slow cooking in the same day. My favorite resource is the *Fix-it and Forget-it Cookbook*.

True Confession

My other method for cooking less often has become a standard household joke around here; I relied on Costco lasagna, salad mixes, etc. See, I'm not too embarrassed to confess it! I'm being brutally honest, here. My best meals have come from Costco—especially as the kids got older and their activities took us away from home more often, I began to rely heavily on Costco meals. Sadly, I can't do this as much anymore. You won't believe this, but when you don't have children at home, it's possible for the Costco-sized chicken to get freezer burn before you can use it up.

My children cooked for themselves in college and regularly shopped at Costco. At the beginning of every week, they put meals in the freezer. They can cook for themselves *and* they earned stellar grades, because they learned to cook as little as possible, too!

I apologize to all my friends who grind their own wheat and cook organic foods. I hope you won't hold it against me!

Chapter 9

Putting it Together

Scheduling needs to be a priority for your homeschool, not only to make things run more smoothly but also to protect you, the teaching parent, from needless stress and overwork. A schedule can remind you to spread out the required work among your spouse and children. Education is not about sitting and being spoon-fed eight hours a day; it is about life. Learning through doing is more effective than learning through listening.

Studies show that 70 percent of effective learning comes through experiential doing, 20 percent through relationships and coaching, and only 10 percent through formal training.

Seek to craft your homeschool schedule with this in mind. Do you want your kids to know how to keep a house? Schedule time for it. Do you want them to understand the value of a dollar? Schedule time for them to work, save money, and work on a budget. Balance doing, coaching, and learning.

Remember to rotate tasks often. Variety is the spice of life and the flavor of homeschooling! Mix desk time with active time. Mix up chores, meals, and activities. Make it a point to experience new things regularly. Keeping your kids energized about learning takes some work. When a strategy you have used in the past is starting to lose effectiveness, change it up. Your schedule is your servant not your taskmaster!

Above all, remember to schedule margin in your homeschool. The white space around your day will enable you to have the perspective to notice when something isn't working anymore. Being too busy is the enemy of productivity and happiness.

Slow down. Let your child slow down. Education isn't a race, it is a lifestyle. No one is served if, at the end of your homeschooling career, your kids hate learning and want to escape the pressure cooker of your homeschool.

Don't fill your homeschool day from edge to edge so you have no room to maneuver. You need quiet time each day to take stock and think about what is working and what isn't. Homeschooling is like a marathon—you need to pace yourself and take regular hydration breaks or you will burn out.

Your homeschool can be successful and even fun! If it isn't currently, share this book with your spouse and have an open discussion on what changes you can make to relieve the stress, share the burden, and put the fun back into your days. You will be so glad you did!

Appendix 1

Cubbies, Tubbies, and Binder Queens

Regardless of whether you are a perfectly organized homeschool mom or not, you've probably given some thought about high school records. Whether you feel the panic, want to stick your head in the sand, or are confident about planning and your ability to carry it out, it's important for every homeschool parent to consider record keeping in high school.

Perhaps it's only a vague thought, saying to yourself, "I'll get to that someday." But time has a way of sneaking up on you. Even if you are convinced your student will never go to college, chances are high that at some point in the future you will need to provide records of your student's high school experience. You may need records for your child to become a camp counselor, or to get a good student discount. After high school, these records might be needed for a job application, graduate school, or as an employment requirement for a job they desire, even 10 years from now. Homeschool records will ensure you'll always be prepared.

Forgetting Large Chunks of Information

Record keeping is so important because it's completely possible for a normal homeschool parent to accidentally forget large chunks of information. A few years ago, I was working on a transcript with a mom named Paula. She thought her transcript would be easy because she had been keeping records. In truth, her record keeping book was completely empty. We had to work through old receipts and curriculum records to create her child's transcript. We didn't worry though, we simply discussed every subject area in detail, from algebra to American Sign Language.

Once the records were complete, she was so happy! As I was leaving, I asked, "What are you doing this weekend?" Paula didn't hesitate for a moment, explaining they were going to a Latin competition.

"Latin competition?" I said. "You never mentioned Latin!" That was how I discovered that her high school junior had already completed four years of high school Latin, and her mother had completely forgotten about it. A very large and important part of her homeschool was completely missing from her transcript, and would have stayed that way if I hadn't asked about her weekend plans. Now it's not as if four years of Latin was a repressed memory of something horribly traumatic. It was obvious the student enjoyed Latin—that's why she was still competing, and why they were both looking forward to the weekend.

You need to keep high school records. Keeping records will help you remember your homeschool experiences so you can create great transcripts and course descriptions. Record keeping is important so you don't forget broad swaths of learning, such as four years of Latin.

Keep high school records so you can make a transcript that reflects the courses you taught and so you don't short-change your student. Paula is a gifted home educator and loving mother, who did an exceptional job homeschooling her children, yet even she forgot four years of Latin. Never underestimate the human ability to forget, because it can happen to anyone!

You can avoid a record keeping crisis of your own. Learn how to keep high school records, so this doesn't happen to you.

Choose a Record Keeping Style

There are four basic methods of homeschool record keeping.

Tubbies

Some parents keep all their homeschool records in a giant plastic tub in the school room. I call these parents "tubbies." They keep all their children's records in one single tub. All tests, assignments and papers are lovingly tossed in the top, awaiting the blessed someday when they magically become organized. Tubbies keep a lot of homeschool stuff but lack organization. Still, you can create some high school records even if you are keeping records like a tubby.

Cubbies

Slightly more organized are "cubbies." As in a Kindergarten class, where each student has their own cubby, these moms use the same strategy for record keeping. They keep records in an enclosed cupboard, cabinet, or drawer. Slightly more organized than tubbies, cubbies usually have one drawer for each child and sometimes for each year as well. Cubbies keep many records with minimal organization, but at least they can tell which child did the work on each paper, since each child's records have their own designated place.

Binder Queens

Even more organized are "binder queens." They are the parents who keep notebooks filled with records—one child per notebook. These parents keep track of student work in highly organized, divider-filled spiral notebooks, binders, computer programs, or spreadsheets. Some fancier binder queens have a designer file folder with a carry handle. Binder queens keep information on every class, which can help them easily create records for all classes. At homeschool conventions, I can spot these parents from a mile away, with their business-like notebook and list of questions in hand. They tend to be the most organized people I meet. True confession—I was a binder queen.

Question Marks

The final type of homeschool parents are the ones I affectionately refer to as "question marks." When this type of parent hears about record keeping, an invisible question mark appears over their ever-so-slightly-cocked head as they think to themselves, "Records? Were we supposed to keep records?" This is the one method of record keeping I simply can't condone. It's just a bad idea to stick your head in the sand, hoping that record keeping isn't important. You can easily lose something significant, such as four years of Latin, Eagle Scout experiences, or other key ingredients needed to create your child's transcript and course descriptions.

Each homeschool parent will decide which method is best for them. And of course, no record keeping method will work unless you use the record keeping method you choose. I usually recommend that parents try to get more organized each year. If you are a tubby the first year, try to graduate to a cubby the next year. Move up the food chain!

Become a Binder Queen

Being a binder queen requires a minimal investment. A few dollars will get you everything you need: a 3-ring binder, a set of dividers, and some notebook paper. All it requires is a few minutes each week, making sure the binder is prepared and used instead of ignored. Using a binder system is a convenient way to keep work samples and graded work from every class. If colleges ever want to see something from Latin or

Macroeconomics class, simply reach into the binder for a work sample.

Simple is better. My binders were three inch, 3-ring binders, each with a simple label such as "Kevin 20X8-20X9." At the beginning of the year, label each divider in the binder. In the front of the binder, label a section for the transcript. Then arrange a section for everything required by your state law. You might include a divider for your Declaration of Intent to Homeschool, immunization records, or annual testing records.

Next, label a divider for each class you intend to teach. This includes English, math, social studies, science, foreign language, physical education, fine art, and electives for the year. You can record test scores or grades for each lab or report on a simple piece of notebook paper. Store significant papers behind each divider to keep as work samples.

You don't need to keep everything, but it

can be helpful to keep papers that you evaluated. Later in the year, perhaps in the spring, go back over what you learned and develop a course description for each class. If you started a class but didn't finish, just throw that divider away; there's no reason to record what was not covered.

Keeping a place for my records helped me to keep my records up to date. Every month I gathered all the papers my kids produced and gradually filled up each 3-ring binder. As the year progressed, I could see which sections were filling up and which sections were blank. Once the blank sections were identified, I could concentrate on developing records for those sections. When the art divider was empty, I assigned my children a one page paper on an artist. When the music section was blank, I had them list their performance-ready piano pieces and added their Christmas Recital program to it.

Keep Homeschool Records

Record keeping is different from scrapbooking—it's not an artistic endeavor. Keep high school level academic records. There are three big high school record keeping categories.

1. Keep anything required by your state homeschool law. This may include a declaration of intent to homeschool or an immunization record.

2. Keep what you will need for college admission. Be prepared, because you don't always know what the future will hold.

3. Keep records needed to create course descriptions and a high school transcript. You are the high school, so you are in charge of these records.

It's relatively simple for many classes. Keep any tests or papers your child has written, and you're done! For other classes, you may want to keep lab reports, tests, research papers, or short essays. Some classes don't include paper assignments, and record keeping will require some creativity. The credit value of courses such as P.E., fine arts, and other electives may be hard to quantify unless you keep track of hours. You can also make a list of the activities completed or resources used in each class.

One mother asked what records she should keep for her child learning how to cook at home. Think outside the box, and consider what your child does to learn. This child created a menu, went grocery shopping, and cooked using recipes. These are all great homeschool records! Save the menu, the shopping list, and photocopy recipes for culinary arts class records.

There are many other ways to keep records. Keep a printout of the curriculum you purchase. List every book your child buys, uses, or reads for pleasure. Track hours spent on subjects, projects, or activities that aren't bookish. Keep online descriptions from internet or co-op classes. Photocopy textbook covers and table of contents. Keep any assignment sheets or schedules you create.

Instead of writing down what you want your child to do in the future, you can write down what your child did after the work is completed. (This will help parents who are conscientious, but not good at planning ahead.) Have your child keep a journal of school work, including books, assignments, and experiences. Most students do some of their work on the computer, so be careful to save it in a school file on the computer or printed out in your filing box, or both.

Create High School Documents

Once every spring, create and update the important high school documents you will need to demonstrate your child's awesome home education.

1. Transcript

Plan to create an Official Transcript. This is a simple Word document, created on your home computer, with the words "Official Transcript" in the title.

2. Course descriptions

Each class description should have three main ingredients. First, write a descriptive paragraph about what you did. This is a simple fifth grade writing assignment, not a college thesis, so don't over-think it. Second, include a list of what you used, from textbooks to supplements or experiences. Third, describe how you graded or evaluated, remembering that there should be more than merely tests to influence your final grade.

3. Reading and award lists

Make a list of the books read each year. This is easier when you keep all your library and curriculum purchase receipts each year. Keep a list of the activities your child is involved in and the awards or volunteer hours they earned in each activity.

When to Keep Records

Keep records early. Record keeping is not a switch that you can suddenly turn on; it can help to practice. I started training myself to keep records when my children were in seventh grade so I would be competent by the time they were in high school. If your child is in seventh or eighth grade, practice keeping your homeschool records as if they were already in high school, to be prepared for anything as you move forward. It's common for homeschoolers to do some high school level work in middle school.

Keep records often. It's a rare person who updates homeschool records every day, but every parent can manage keeping up with records every month or two. As you train yourself to keep records, strive to keep something to document every subject your child learns.

Keep records in high school. Homeschool records become critical once a student begins high school as they are part of the transcript that will be shared with colleges. Begin the transcript as soon as your child is in 9th grade, or at age 14. Update the transcript and course descriptions every spring from 9th through 12th grade, until high school is complete.

Start Today

Right now, it's time for a decision. Decide whether you will be a tubby, cubby, or binder queen (or king) this year. At a minimum, grab a big box and put it in your schoolroom to collect everything. Or buy a cubby system with drawers, with one drawer per child per year. Or invest the big bucks and get a 3-ring binder at the dollar store, with dividers for each subject area.

Prepare throughout the school year and spend some concentrated time collecting records for your homeschooled high schooler. Create documents that will impress a college or employer. Try to move up the record keeping food chain, improving over the years so that by the time your student is a senior, their transcripts and course descriptions are organized and prepared. Start small, but start somewhere!

Today is the day to begin! Ready? Go!

Appendix 2

iTired – Dealing with Homeschool Fatigue

Fatigue is an epic battle for homeschool parents. Often, it's the biggest issue that homeschoolers face in the middle of winter. Between homeschooling and housework, parents feel stretched. Add your own need for self-care, the needs of your children and spouse, and it can feel impossible. Then add the darkness of winter months, and even seasoned veterans can be hanging on by a thread.

Yes, it's easy to become overwhelmed and fatigued! But there are some solutions that will help you face the day bravely, with the confidence and energy you need to make it through the year . . . or at least until dinnertime. Hey, some ideas might even get you into the evening hours without a meltdown.

Put Priorities First

Every homeschool parent has a subject they don't understand, tolerate, like, or even remember to teach. When you identify your weak area, you can do something about it!

Once you have identified your weak subject, remember to put that subject *first*—it's the first thing your student does in the morning and then it's out of the way! You're not spending all day worrying about it or nagging your child to get that dreaded subject done!

Make sure it's always done and never missed. Prioritize it by also spending extra time and money on the weak area. A monetary investment in these weak areas has two potential benefits. First, it is human nature to value things more if we invest in them. The act of spending money can give you a lift in attitude. The second benefit is, believe it or not, you may purchase something that could make the dreaded topic more tolerable and, dare I say . . . fun! This strategy can eliminate a lot of stress and help prevent homeschool fatigue.

Hold a Morning Meeting

If you tend to fall behind, or if you see your student becoming overwhelmed by their work, instituting a "Morning Meeting" can be the perfect answer!

It's so easy for children to get off-track. Teenagers often seem to have an uncanny ability to avoid work. That's where the Morning Meeting idea can help begin the process of helping your kids become responsible adults.

When you check on your child each day, you can shape and mold their "responsibility index." A quick 15 or 30-minute check-in can give you the time you need to assess the situation and correct the behavior, shaping and molding your child's responsibility as you go. Try having a quick morning meeting for a successful and less stressful homeschool!

Enjoy Your Coffee

A cup of coffee or tea can be your inspiration for homeschool happiness. It can motivate you to hold your morning meeting with your kids.

When you meet with your child each day, and go over your expectations for them, the whole day will go more smoothly. A quick daily check-in is often all it takes.

It reminds me a lot of having a quiet time. Your morning coffee can help you have your morning meeting with God. When you meet with the Lord each day, and He reveals His expectations for you, then your whole day will go more smoothly. A quick daily check-in with the Bible can be the encouragement you need to stay on course.

Coffee can encourage you to take care of yourself. If you do some self-care, you'll be much more capable of doing some other-care. We do so much for others all day long. A little bit of "me time" can start the day off right.

It doesn't have to be coffee, it can be tea or a warm meal, but taking care of you is the first step toward taking care of others. Remember what the airlines say, "first put on your own oxygen mask."

Coffee can encourage budding friendships if you can plan a coffee date with another homeschool mom. Instead of dropping your child off at a play date, stay and enjoy fellowship with others. We often crave the company of someone other than our children, and sharing a coffee can encourage sharing our feelings.

The best support system I had was my weekly cup of coffee with my best friend. She shared her struggles with learning disabilities, and I shared my woes with my own children. We both ended up with a better appreciation for the struggles others face.

Coffee can ensure margin. Everyone needs time in their day when nothing is planned. The margin of your day is like the margin in a book. Book margins make a book readable, like life margins make life livable.

If you don't have time to sit down for a cup of coffee, then you don't have enough margin in your life. Take a moment. Sip. Breathe. It's cheaper than therapy.

Your quiet moments of relaxation can give wonderful memories. I remember going to Starbucks once a week, while my son Kevin taught chess. It was Alex and me in the coffee shop; he was studying and I was sipping my peppermint mocha learning about homeschooling high school. Good memories.

Invest in Self Care

A healthy body is less fatigued, and more resistant to disease. To fight fatigue, eat healthy food and get regular rest at night. When you are tired, especially during seasons when you can't sleep all night, be sure to take a nap.

Care for yourself, because your job is so important, and your children are counting on you to be healthy, rested, and responsive. This can't happen if you are exhausted, fatigued, or overly frustrated.

Care for yourself by scheduling some free time each day. Spend time with other moms. Share feelings with trustworthy friends. Having enough time to yourself will mean you can't do it all alone. Delegate some responsibilities to your spouse and children. Delegation is not a sign of weakness; it's the sign of a leader. You are the leader of your home, and it's your job to delegate some tasks.

A healthy spiritual life can fight fatigue as well, giving you a sense of purpose and value. Have a regular quiet time each day, reading the Bible. Spend time praying and verbalizing your reliance on God as your source of strength.

Move More

Get your blood pumping and you'll stay awake. Do something to increase your blood flow. Little things can get that heart rate up. Regularly change your study location, moving from kitchen, to couch, to desk.

Take regular breaks. Between books, or between courses, take a few minutes off. Take five minutes to put in a load of laundry or empty the dishwasher. Sure, it's only housework, but it's still a break from studying and teaching, and sometimes that's all you need.

Drink a glass of water each hour. This will certainly get you up and moving more (at least to the bathroom!) and can increase your circulation.

Exercise can battle fatigue. Set aside time to exercise regularly. Perhaps you can exercise in the morning, before school starts. Maybe you can exercise in the afternoon, when older teens or your spouse can supervise quiet seatwork.

Take a quick walk. If you can't exercise, then take a stroll around the yard or neighborhood, and don't call it exercise. Go outside and breathe the fresh air. A brisk walk, no matter how long or how short, can be rejuvenating, or at least wake you up enough to get your work done. Going outside is often the real cure for fatigue.

Vary the Routine

Once a day, try to mix in some fun activities. You might do a creative project or a hands-on activity. A fun activity might be a science experiment, an art project, or playing a musical instrument.

Anything that is different from reading a book can provide stimulation. Try to do one creative or hands-on activity each day. During seatwork time, you can vary the routine by adding music.

Once a week, make it your goal to play. Really play. Schedule something fun to do and get out of the house. For some families, this might be a long trip to town for groceries, but taking a quick stop for fun at the park.

Another family might schedule a sports activity or meeting with friends each week. If you plan one day away from home, it won't mess up your schedule or keep you from completing your duties.

On the other hand, if you are always running around, you don't need to do more playing than already planned. This playtime doesn't have to take all day—an hour or so can make all the difference.

Once a month, consider taking a mental health day. Everyone feels as if they can't take it anymore sometimes. It's not a sign of weakness to need a day off.

Schools regularly plan for mid-winter breaks because they know it's hard to stay focused during the dark months of winter. Take a break and give yourself a day off when you need it. People who work hard know the value of a true day of rest.

Find a Coping Mechanism

Sitting back to relax with a warm cup of coffee or tea can help you relax and take care of yourself. My way of coping may not fit everyone. Create your own coping mechanism.

I was leading a discussion of coping mechanisms on Facebook. "How do you cope with homeschool fatigue?" I got so many great suggestions, you are sure to find something that will help you today! Here are the great ideas other homeschoolers suggested.

Which suggestion will work for you today?

"Change location, sunshine works best, Food throughout the day, coffee, yogurt fruit smoothies from blender, fresh carrot apple juice from juicer, breakfast, mid-morning snack, lunch, happy hour favorite fruit juice with cheese dip and tortilla chips, dinner, dessert. Run in the morning, walk the dog mid-day and before bed to find time alone with hubby, bike ride, whenever possible . . . seeking healthy options." ~ Laura

"Exercise! I go for a walk alone every day once the school day is done. It's a great way for me to downshift from homeschool mom, teacher, principal, guidance counselor mode into a more relaxed 'just mom' mode." ~ Sonja

"Spending time with other homeschool moms. It refreshes my soul."~ Laura

"To prevent burnout, I build some cushion into our schedule, allowing for one or two impromptu days off each month. I limit our outside activities while also trying to have at least one Sanity Day (full day at home) each week. Then if life gets too hectic or we are still facing burnout, I drop everything except the absolute essentials for a few days: reading great books, notebooking, basic math, and lots of nature study." ~ Rebecca

"Drop the "studies" for a day, two or three, or a week, to play, relax, go to the park, and regroup. My kids love to color, so sometimes we just print a pile of coloring pages or paper dolls, let them create or play games, put on music or audio books and yes, naps are great if you can squeeze them in. I guess my biggest strategy is really to do all of those things before any burnout sets it -

like sometimes a rainy day is just a cozy day to relax." ~ Galadriel

"Change of location. When we feel burnt out, we pack things up and study somewhere else. For us, that's usually the park. We sit in the car to read or do seat work. Then, they can play for a while (P.E.) before we head back. Sometimes we do nature walks for science, even if it doesn't go with that year's subject. Or, we take a field trip somewhere close. Though, I am working on getting better at field trips." ~ Carrie

"Taking probiotics at bedtime. And making sure I spend time with The Lord each day reading His word, definitely gives me a new perspective on things." ~ Heidi

"We take breaks every six weeks. We put the curriculum away and focus on our other interests like art, movies, video games, shopping with friends, etc. There is still plenty of learning going on during this relaxed time." ~ Michelle

"Attending daily mass is a reminder for why I have children and why it is my responsibility to educate them. Thanks to God for the blessings He has given our family. I have two awesome teenage boys!" ~ Happy

"Going outside really helps me when I'm stressed or tired but still need to get school done. We have a hammock chair that I love or sometimes I just spread a sheet & bring a pillow." ~ Suzanne

"A quick workout during lunch break. And a big glass of water." ~ Sherry

"Bible lessons and drinking Virgil's Root Beer or Black Cherry Cream Soda." ~ Piety

"Chocolate with coffee. Taking a day off on occasion helps us all feel better. I can do chores, and my daughter can do whatever she feels like." ~ Stephanie

"While standing still and waiting on son to do a task, I have started to exercise: squats, leg kicks, do the grapevine, back kicks, walking in place, etc. Not only am I getting exercise, it is making me feel better and have more energy. GET MOVING!!" ~ Susan

"Park days with friends." ~ Jennifer

"Very important to spend time in prayer and bible study. Also, very important to have a time by yourself at least once a week." ~ Sandi

"Prayer and a white board with simple tasks that can be crossed off—helps me stay on target when too tired to hold it in my head!" ~ Debbie

"After lessons are done (and if I can swing it) I take a 30-minute nap. Also like to go outside with the brood for a walk." ~ Heather

"I've been homeschooling for 15+ years now with multiple children. Here are

some of things I've learned to combat fatigue: 1) Delegate, delegate, delegate. Mom does not have to do everything. 2) Perfectionism leads to fatigue. You, your house, your kids and your husband do not need to be perfect. 3) Plan time to take care of yourself. It's imperative to take care of your health. If you aren't healthy, it makes it difficult to take care of others. 4) Laugh . . . often. The kids have created a disaster in the family room, you burned dinner, and the baby just puked down your back. You can laugh, cry or get angry. Choose to laugh. It's really easy to get angry or cry. It takes an effort to look for the positives. Make the effort. You'll be happier about it and feel less burned out in general."
~ Erika

"Changing location. Move to the living room, kitchen, park, backyard, etc."
~ Cindy

"We have SOS days. (Save Our Sanity). A random day off studies to go out and enjoy nature, or to watch old movies all day, or make stuff, or cook fun things we wouldn't normally make, etc. It's more for my sanity than theirs, but they do appreciate it." ~ Heidi

"1. Switch it up and plan a fun lesson. 2. Take a picnic lunch break, followed by a nature walk. 3. Use educational DVDs or audio books every so often. 4. Have an older child help a younger one. 5. Read poetry. It's soothing. 6. Keep on praying! 7. Don't let fear or guilt weigh you down. 8. Eat a healthy breakfast. 9. Finish your work in four days, and make Friday an enrichment day. 10. You will be tired from time to time. Just do what you can." ~ Heather

"Do one thing creative each day... arrange some flowers... drop someone a SHORT note... pull together one page to scrapbook later... pull together things for a handmade greeting card... bake something to give to a neighbor. I'm in my 17th or 18th year of homeschooling and still struggle with tiredness at times." ~ Connie

"Definitely taking a day off to go do something fun. We have picture day in the fall, ice skating in the winter and sometimes we'll curl up with mugs of hot goodies and watch a movie. Moms need to have something that they enjoy doing and it doesn't have to be away from home. Having a definite stop and start time for school helps too and them you won't feel like that's all you do." ~ Tricia

"Nap! Have realistic expectations. Spend time with like-minded friends who can encourage you." ~ Mary Jo

"Don't be afraid to ditch curriculum that is just not working (or just take a break from it and rethink approach). Do things that you love to do as a family to recharge everyone's batteries."~ Gail

"Praise music always helps me to power through it! Usually a day off to rest or catch up also alleviates some of the fatigue." ~ Autismland

"Delegating and asking for help are big ones (and hard to remember for me). Taking time off is also important. My hubby used to often walk in from work, look at my face, and send me to Books a Million for a cream soda and a book." ~ Tina

"When I need a break I exclaim, "Time for P.E.!" and send the kids to the backyard until further notice." ~ Ivette

"Most important things. For housework and for homeschool, I always have in mind what are the most important things, both for the long term and for the day, for each child. That way, if I don't get anything else done, I know I've done the things that matter most." ~ Rebecca

"Mani/pedi - so worth the $. Makes you feel like a girl (not just a mom)." ~ Theresa

"A day of scriptures, and fasting prayer, to ponder each child and then record inspirations or personal revelations I receive. I notice for our family, burn out only happens when we lose sight or get off track of what we were inspired to do in the first place. Amazing how easy it is to lose track of what is working, and slip into 'other things.'" ~ Brenda

Afterword

Who is Lee Binz and What Can She Do for Me?

Number one best-selling homeschool author, Lee Binz is The HomeScholar. Her mission is "helping parents homeschool high school." Lee and her husband, Matt, homeschooled their two boys, Kevin and Alex, from elementary through high school.

Upon graduation, both boys received four-year, full tuition scholarships from their first choice university. This enables Lee to pursue her dream job—helping parents homeschool their children through high school.

On The HomeScholar website, you will find great products for creating homeschool transcripts and comprehensive records to help you amaze and impress colleges.

Find out why Andrew Pudewa, Founder of the Institute for Excellence in Writing says, "Lee Binz knows how to navigate this often confusing and frustrating labyrinth better than anyone."

You can find Lee online at:

HomeHighSchoolHelp.com

If this book has been helpful, could you please take a minute to write us a quick review on Amazon? Thank you!

Testimonials

Lee Binz is a genius at taking complex information and making it simple. She simplified the information in a fun and quite comical way. I felt so empowered! I now have the information I need to turn what my children enjoy doing into credits on their transcript. I highly recommend visiting her website and purchasing her books!

~ Monica

Sooo, I asked for feedback on my son's high school transcripts I submitted for early college. Since this is my first time homeschooling all the way through, I was pleased to hear these words: "You did an incredible job in putting everything together; the transcript, the course descriptions, the book list and report card. It's very professional and detailed. Typically, more information is better than less. When I first saw the records, I thought it was a private school." Thank you, Lee Binz for all your help!

~Lisa

For more information about my Comprehensive Record Solution and Gold Care Club, go to:

ComprehensiveRecordSolution.com and GoldCareClub.com

Also From The HomeScholar...

- The HomeScholar Guide to College Admission and Scholarships: Homeschool Secrets to Getting Ready, Getting In and Getting Paid (Book and Kindle Book)

- Setting the Records Straight—How to Craft Homeschool Transcripts and Course Descriptions for College Admission and Scholarships (Book and Kindle Book)

- TechnoLogic: How to Set Logical Technology Boundaries and Stop the Zombie Apocalypse

- Finding the Faith to Homeschool High School

- The Easy Truth About Homeschool Transcripts (Kindle Book)

- Parent Training A la Carte (Online Training)

- Total Transcript Solution (Online Training, Tools and Templates)

- Comprehensive Record Solution (Online Training, Tools and Templates)

- Gold Care Club (Comprehensive Online Support and Training)

- Silver Training Club (Online Training)

The HomeScholar Coffee Break Books Released or Coming Soon on Kindle and Paperback:

- Delight Directed Learning: Guiding Your Homeschooler Toward

Passionate Learning

- Creating Transcripts for Your Unique Child: Help Your Homeschool Graduate Stand Out from the Crowd

- Beyond Academics: Preparation for College and for Life

- Planning High School Courses: Charting the Course Toward High School Graduation

- Graduate Your Homeschooler in Style: Make Your Homeschool Graduation Memorable

- Keys to High School Success: Get Your Homeschool High School Started Right!

- Getting the Most Out of Your Homeschool This Summer: Learning just for the Fun of it!

- Finding a College: A Homeschooler's Guide to Finding a Perfect Fit

- College Scholarships for High School Credit: Learn and Earn With This Two-for-One Strategy!

- College Admission Policies Demystified: Understanding Homeschool Requirements for Getting In

- A Higher Calling: Homeschooling High School for Harried Husbands (by Matt Binz, Mr. HomeScholar)

- Gifted Education Strategies for Every Child: Homeschool Secrets for Success

- College Application Essays: A Primer for Parents

- Creating Homeschool Balance: Find Harmony Between Type A and Type Zzz . . .

- Homeschooling the Holidays: Sanity Saving Strategies and Gift Giving Ideas

- Your Goals this Year: A Year by Year Guide to Homeschooling High School

- Making the Grades: A Grouch-Free Guide to Homeschool Grading

- High School Testing: Knowledge That Saves Money

- Getting the BIG Scholarships: Learn Expert Secrets for Winning College Cash!

- Easy English for Simple Homeschooling: How to Teach, Assess and Document High School English

- Scheduling—The Secret to Homeschool Sanity: Plan You Way Back to Mental Health

- Junior Year is the Key to High School Success: How to Unlock the Gate to Graduation and Beyond

- Upper Echelon Education: How to Gain Admission to Elite Universities

- How to Homeschool College: Save Time, Reduce Stress and Eliminate Debt

- Homeschool Curriculum That's Effective and Fun: Avoid the Crummy Curriculum Hall of Shame!

- Comprehensive Homeschool Records: Put Your Best Foot Forward to Win College Admission and Scholarships

- Options After High School: Steps to Success for College or Career

- How to Homeschool 9th and 10th Grade: Simple Steps for Starting Strong!

- Senior Year Step-by-Step: Simple Instructions for Busy Homeschool Parents

- How-to-Homeschool Independently: Do-it-Yourself Secrets to Rekindle the Love of Learning

- High School Math The Easy Way: Simple Strategies for Homeschool Parents in Over Their Heads

- Homeschooling Middle School with Powerful Purpose: How to Successfully Navigate 6th through 8th Grade

- Simple Science for Homeschooling High School: Because Teaching Science isn't Rocket Science!

Would you like to be notified when we offer the next Coffee Break Books for FREE during our Kindle promotion days? If so, leave your name and email below and we will send you a reminder.

HomeHighSchoolHelp.com/
freekindlebook

Visit my Amazon Author Page!

amazon.com/author/leebinz

Made in the USA
Columbia, SC
24 January 2022

54109584R00070